Handwritten inscription: "KLARKE THANK YOU MAY THE FORCE BE WITH YOU! [signature] 2011"

Picture Your ESP!

REVEAL YOUR HIDDEN POWERS WITH *THE NU ESP TEST*

Alain Nu
The Man Who Knows™

Library of Congress Cataloging-in-Publication Data
Library of Congress Catalog Number: 2010926284
Copyright © 2010 Nu Magiconcepts, LLC
ISBN-10: 0-9842085-2-6
ISBN-13: 978-0-9842085-2-4

Layout & Typography by Sarah Sorden (www.sarahsloth.com)

Edited by Tanya Thielke

Photograph Credits: Peter Austin, Kevin Creaghan, Fredde Lieberman, Tom Magliery, Douglas Moors, D. Sharon Pruitt, TJ Scott, Leya Tesmenitsky, Tanya Thielke, Gary Thomas, David Waldman, Reginna Zhidov, Earl Zubkoff.

Publisher: CFBP Bestsellers
An imprint of CFB Productions, Inc.
P. O. Box 50008, Henderson, NV 89016
www.CFBPBestsellers.com

dedication

To Tanya and Nico, the most intuitive people in my world.

acknowledgements

Special thanks to everyone who helped or inspired me to create this book:

Adega Wine Cellars & Café

John Alexander

Simon Aronson

Lee Asher

Peter Austin

John Bannon

Joey Burton

Kevin Creaghan

Madam's Organ Blues Bar

Clinton Ford Billups, Jr.

Bob Cassidy

Mark Chorvinsky

Doug Dyment

Jerome Finley

Sam Haine

Matthew and Wendy Lesko

Fredde Lieberman

Tom Magliery

Mike Meadows

Douglas Moors

Nico Nu

The Psychic Entertainers Association

D. Sharon Pruitt

T.J. Scott

Sarah Sorden

Leya Tesmenitsky

Tanya Thielke

Gary Thomas

Dai Vernon

David Waldman

Reginna Zhidov

Earl Zubkof

4

table of contents

About the Author 7

Why I created *The Nu ESP Test* 9

How to Use this Book 11

Chapter 1: Headspace 13

Chapter 2: Simple Psigns 23

Chapter 3: How Psi I Am 35

Chapter 4: Paranormal Thinking 45

Chapter 5: Funny Feelings 59

Chapter 6: Sixth Sense 69

Chapter 7: Awareness 81

Your Psychic Score and What it Means 89

Why Test Your ESP? 93

Final Thoughts 94

Now What? 95

Suggested Reading 97

about the author

Alain Nu's lifelong passion for mysterious and unknown realms was formed in his early childhood. Growing up in San Francisco in the 1970's, Alain was exposed at an early age to the world of fortunetellers, street performers and other practitioners of the "mystery arts." Like many children, his mind was agile and creative. He was fascinated by paleontology and became an avid and knowledgeable young rock collector. Largely shunned by his peers for somehow being "different," he turned his natural desire to connect with others inwards. With two hard-working parents and little outside community, he befriended neighborhood animals and regularly "walked" with a pack of free-running dogs that seemed to flock to his magnetic energy. This experience of friendship beyond species had a definite impact on his belief that a "force" of sorts connects all living things in the universe.

His parents' decision to move to Washington, DC, cemented his destiny through a process of personal struggle and triumph. At the time, being the only Asian student in his new school, he was now ostracized by others to an even greater degree than before. Operating completely outside social cliques and other mainstays of childhood to adolescent life, he spent his time honing his skills in magic and esoteric studies.

As a youth, his interest in the unknown manifested in anything he could research, and/or get away with—basement séances, UFO clubs, and playfully testing he and his friends' psychic ability with playing cards. He asked his father who worked at the Library of Congress to bring home hard-to-find books on magic, strange phenomena and parapsychology so he could learn as much as possible about these topics. He became close friends with and worked for Mark Chorvinsky, publisher/editor of *Strange Magazine*, which covered many topics of the weird and unexplained. Connecting with this new world of people consumed with a passion for pursuing the unknown on so many different levels brought Alain's personal sense of the importance of these topics to a new level. Eventually, Alain's interest turned towards the field of "mentalism"—parlor demonstrations of ESP, mind reading and telekinesis.

The path on which he found himself seemed to be his only true calling, and Alain came to the moment of decision on which his entire future depended. To Alain, there was no question that he was already doing exactly what he needed to do. Against tremendous odds, he built a career that eventually brought him to headline at Caesars Palace in Las Vegas and star in four of his own hour-long television specials: "The Mysterious World of Alain Nu" which aired on TLC and international television. His endless creativity and high standard of excellence over many years earned him several awards, along with the deep respect and admiration of his peers.

Always trying to keep up with the latest studies on the brain and consciousness, Alain's interest was piqued by recent findings linking quantum physics and serious parapsychological research. Invigorated by the implications of these parallel fields of study, Alain's role became clearer than ever: To develop programs that introduce ordinary people to their own extraordinary abilities.

Determined to seek his own path as "The Man Who Knows," Alain has intrigued Washington society with his incredible programs of wonder along with the message of furthering one's openness to the marvels of human interconnectivity. Presenting at universities, corporations and association events, Alain gained a wide reputation for entertaining very sophisticated audiences with his uncanny demonstrations that blur the line between science and the mysteries of unexplained phenomena.

In his one-man, touring stage show *Invisible Connections*, Alain Nu utilizes these untold powers to foretell our actions, reveal our unspoken thoughts and create seemingly impossible phenomena. "Nothing is impossible as long as you know how to adjust your perception," says Alain Nu. "Think about it. With just our thoughts and words as tools of visualization, we have the beginnings of untold power."

How does he do it? Alain Nu is reluctant to reveal his Especially Sensitive Powers. He acknowledges that his uncanny abilities may incorporate elements of probability, psychology, suggestion, professional techniques or just plain "good timing." Most importantly, however, he sees himself as a public speaker and entertainer. But taking this all one step further, Alain is quite certain that there is *something more*. And now having developed *The Nu ESP Test*, he feels that this just may open the doors to your own uncanny experiences!

How does he know this? "I feel that each of us has a hidden super-potential that is real," he says. "With *The Nu ESP Test*, I'm hoping to show people that their own intention to develop such powers can indeed be practiced!" says Nu.

Currently working on a new television series and writing several books, Alain resides in the Washington, DC, metro-area with his wife and daughter.

For more information about Alain Nu, please visit: *www.TheManWhoKnows.TV*

why i created
The NU ESP Test

For some time now, a few brave and pioneering scientists have devoted their careers to studying ESP phenomena. Their serious and documented work has accumulated a body of undeniable evidence that in fact there is something about humans and ESP that is very real. In numerous controlled repeatable experiments (which are the foundation of the scientific method) ordinary people have demonstrated the ability to predict an outcome at a success rate that is above chance. Most importantly: the margin is significant enough for established scientists with no career interest in ESP to acknowledge further study is warranted. This means that ESP concepts are gaining, however slowly, a new kind of mainstream acceptance.

And that is exciting to me!

Why?

My career is built on creating live demonstrations that allow people to experience what being psychic or intuitive might feel like. I achieve this by using methods that enable synchronicities to occur at a greater rate than most people would expect. However, over the years I have found myself experiencing moments that even I simply could not account for. Sometimes I seemed just to know something about a person I truly could not have known or even guessed. Other times, people in my audiences would seem simply to know something that I didn't expect.

Like many people, listening to psychic hunches in my personal life, I have noticed that although many can appear trivial, there are a good number of significant ones. A few have even saved my life.

I created this book to give people a fun way to relate to ESP without first having to do extensive research, or attempt to channel past lives or communicate with the deceased. Most people already feel like they have had some kind of ESP experience in their lives, whether it be a hunch, knowing who was going to call them that day, sensing a friend needing help, and so on. I designed the Nu ESP Test as a series of 30 challenges for you to explore your ESP in a casual nonscientific way. For those who want more background on the current state of psi research, you can consult my short suggested reading list near the end of this book.

Throughout this book, we will use the term "psi" (pronounced "sigh") which refers not just ESP, but all paranormal phenomena. Feel free to explore these concepts in any way that feels best for you. While coincidences and synchronicities are fascinating in themselves, I believe a person's intuitive abilities can be developed. And of course I am not alone. People's reasons for wanting to develop these abilities are as varied as people themselves. For most, however, simply experiencing a single ESP phenomenon is reason enough.

10

Photo: Reginna Zhidov AKA "rzhidov" (flickr.com)

how to use this book
READ FIRST

PLEASE READ THIS SECTION FIRST
before looking at the tests. You will have
a more accurate score of your intuitive
abilities at the conclusion of the tests if
none of the pages are looked at in advance.

Each test takes place over two pages. Every
test begins on a right-hand side page
consisting of an image or a photograph
and an instructional meditation. The
following flip side of that page will give
you immediate feedback along with how to
score yourself accordingly. The object of the
"game" here is simply for you to see if you
receive any intuitive information about what
will be revealed in the photograph on the
following page.

Visual images have been used to study
ESP for over a millennium. It seems that
our memories, thoughts and emotional
sensations readily arise from abstract
visuals, and striking photographic images
in particular have a way of bringing forth
strong mental impressions. For this reason,
photographs have been used in ESP
laboratory tests in varying ways which
usually achieve positive results. Once you
understand the manner in which these tests
have been designed, I think it is possible
to practice, develop and continue to test
your intuition and sense of "knowing" on a
casual basis by using a similar template for
testing yourself throughout your life, not
just with other photographs but with events
about to occur.

You will find that concern about your own
belief in your own abilities creates too
much interference. That means not second
guessing yourself, but going with what
feels to be your true instinctive thought. A
"positive energy" and a "quiet mind" are
important to achieving better test results.
Trust your intuitive powers. The better the
knack you have for "knowing," the higher
you will score!

All you need is to:

(1) Be confident,

(2) Relax,

(3) Empty your mind and

(4) Allow yourself to openly "accept"
what flows in to your thoughts.

Try not to contradict what you receive
with your ego or forced imagination.
Often times, it is best to do this in stages.
First, clear your mind of its own ego and
personal needs or concerns; then empty
your thoughts, until you are literally thinking
of nothing. Allow the instructions on each
right-hand page to direct your attention,
and then allow several seconds to pass
so that an intuitive impression organically
forms within your mind that somehow
stands apart from other thoughts. You
may experience it emotionally, or by color,
texture and shape. Sometimes there will
be instructions to write down ALL your
thoughts before turning the page. It's
important for the test that you follow

through with this. It will be used to add up your score points as each result is revealed to you.

Unless instructed, DO NOT consider any of the preceding "meditation" photographs to be psychologically relevant to any of the following page revelations. They are NOT meant to influence the impressions that form in your mind. To experience ESP, the visuals must come from outside these restrictions.

How Psychic Are YOU? The Scoring System:

While no test can perfectly determine how psychic you are, I devised as straightforward a scoring system as possible by determining your odds above chance of getting the answer right. Don't worry - I got an actual statistician to do this job! Each possible answer has a relative point-value to chance and a factor for the degree of the psychic challenge of each test relative to all the others.

To make it easy to add the resulting numbers up, we devised a colored star system corresponding to those point values to allow you to quickly determine your personal psychic "range."

Before taking the test, draw three columns on a piece of a paper, and label them blue, green and red, respectively. When you are given the number of stars for your answer, simply draw a star in the appropriate column. You can make hatch marks too, but stars are more fun! If you want to use three different colored pens, go for it! At the end of your testing you will have an immediate "picture" of where you fall in the psychic spectrum. Red represents the highest level of "inner-knowing,"Blue is still above average, and Green denotes a very possible significant psychic achievement.

If at the end of the tests you see more stars in one column than any other, your psychic abilities may indeed be more weighted in that range. But wait till the very end of the tests before adding anything up. You will be referring to "What your score means" at the end of *The Nu ESP Test* to properly tally your results.

chapter 1:
HEADSPACE

Taking you into the proper "headspace" is the purpose of the first four challenges in this section. They will simply begin to activate your "thinking cap." This is the first step towards sensing and relying on your inner-knowing.

Each challenge takes place over two pages. Beginning on a right-hand page will be an image or a photograph and an instructional meditation. The following flip side of that page will give you immediate feedback along with how to score yourself accordingly. The object of the "game" here is simply for you to see if you receive any intuitive information about what will be revealed in the photograph on the following page.

To achieve this, it is critical that you do not try to analyze why I am asking you to do whatever I instruct you to do. Do not try to find "clues" in the images or photographs that are pictured with each instructional meditation. Your task is to simply "go with your gut."

After writing in your score of each preceding test, take a deep breath. Take about 60 seconds of notes about any mental impressions you may be receiving in that moment, especially if instructed to do so.

You need to be focused, open-minded and most definitely not concerned by whatever your results are. Think of these challenges as exploratory rather than tests to get right or wrong. Just tune into what flows into your mind. It's a good habit, while testing oneself, to take notes of all your impressions. Simply write down as much detail of what you are receiving as you can before turning the page. Make careful note of the correlations between your intuitions and the image and make note of your score, especially if instructed.

You may find yourself doing "better" in the second half of this test than the first, even though the challenge procedure gets more difficult towards the end. If that ends up being the case, this will hopefully boost your confidence that indeed this intuitive ability can be understood more with practice. However, if at the end you find you did not improve or your performance was random, again, don't worry. These challenges are just the first step in a process of engaging your intuition. In any case, at the end of the test, you will tally up your score, analyze your notes, and gain new awareness of your mind's potential.

DFSW
AALM
WANV
AWFK
SSLIRI
PLER
POMD

OAPHADHMOPPPE
FSDZGHIOEPALSS
HIMSNUTROSMOZ
RVLUPNARDICCT
OEDUCIMEIASGNIR
ALMCWQXLZLLKB
KJGNMLBOEWFD

Let's begin by "preparing your brain." Although this first challenge is not necessarily one which scores your intuition per se, the speed at which the answer comes to you may suggest an intuitive process at play. Sometimes it takes a little longer to jumpstart the brain, so don't feel bad if you don't immediately "intuit" the answer. Just relax into it.

Use the second hand of your watch to time yourself.

The letters in red form only two specific words.

See how fast you can unscramble those letters into the two words that appear on the next page.

15

If it took you less than
fifteen seconds to decipher
the words "Storm Drain," give
yourself THREE blue stars.

If it took you more than fifteen, but less
than thirty seconds, give yourself
TWO blue stars.

If it took you more than thirty, but less than one minute,
give yourself ONE blue star.

Now visualize a three letter word…

Keep it clean, though! The word is
not SEX. Also remember not to become
influenced by this preceding image… so the
word I want you to think of is not AIR and it's not
SKY either. Finally, don't think of words like "and" or
"the". Focus on a three letter word that's easy to picture
within your thoughts. Take a few moments for the impression
to form, and turn the page.

Photo: D. Sharon Pruitt (flickr.com)

If you thought of a CAT, give yourself THREE blue stars.

If the image of the cat that came to you was a silhouette OR if an impression you made as a note preceding had significantly matched this photograph in any way, add ONE additional green star.

If you felt your answer was not as significant, but had possible merit, give yourself ONE blue star. Be honest with yourself.

18

Clear your mind. Try to avoid any interfering outside thoughts such as preconceptions, second-guesses and so on.

Just look at my hand and imagine…

How many fingers do you think I am holding up on the next page?

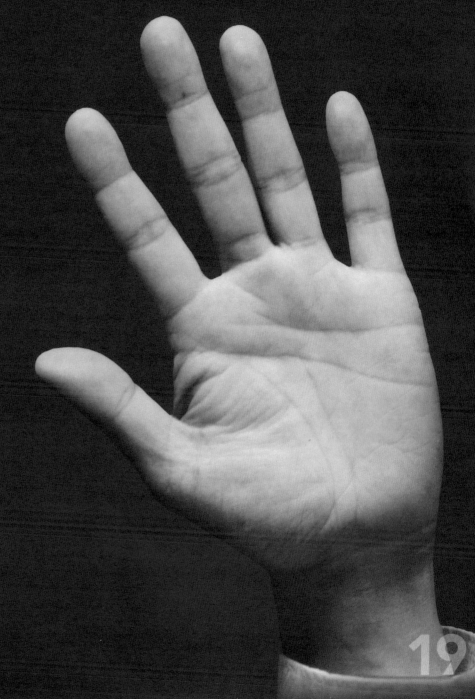

Photo: Fredde Lieberman

If you picked TWO fingers, give yourself TWO blue stars. If you picked one or three, give yourself ONE blue star.

I'll base this one on a curve…

Photo: Fredde Lieberman

This fruit salad consists of four different fruits.

Imagine picking up one piece of fruit and eating it. Write down this first choice. Now imagine eating a different piece of fruit. Make note of this second choice. Finally think of what your third and fourth choice would be and write them down.

Flip the page to see how well you did.

If you got all four correct, give yourself ONE green and THREE blue stars. If you got three, give yourself FOUR blue stars. If you got two correct, give yourself TWO blue stars.

You have passed through the first four challenges of *The Nu ESP Test*. Hopefully you are getting used to this unconventional format, and not feeling too out of your element!

In the next section, in addition to writing down your score, spend an extra minute or so making as many notes of all impressions, images, feelings and sensations that may come to you. Between three and seven random impressions is fine. Let them simply "surface in your mind." Don't worry if they seem trivial or even unrelated entirely to what is being asked. If items from your daily "to-do list" pop into your head, write them down also so that they will not continue to interfere with your process of concentration.

The faster you write and the more "free flowing" any random words are written, the better this works. This is called *automatic writing*. These notes will be used to see if any premonitions of the following test photos or even actual events correlate with them.

chapter 2:
SIMPLE PSIGNS

At this point you are probably experiencing some increased awareness about how your mind "feels." You might be experiencing some confusion between which of the multiple thoughts and images coming your way are the ones that seem to have that "gut feeling." As you move into the next set of challenges, allow your mind to further relax and ease into this new territory.

People who report having precognitive experiences often describe the way it feels as unquestionably true. In other words, without analysis or without a train of thought leading to an image or piece of knowledge, the knowledge is just there and feels complete with no explanation as to why. These compelling moments stand out from the rest of the normal daily ebb and flow of thoughts and experiences of the mind. We'll call these moments "knowing without knowing."

Because you are going through this book, you will naturally be experiencing something a little different from the above because you are aware that you are "testing" this ability. This self-consciousness is what you will be attempting to bypass so you can tap into an intuitive moment of feeling something truly different. This difference can be very subtle, so let your self-consciousness simply rest and allow your mind to display its images and thoughts almost like a movie that you are passively watching.

While it should really take you no longer than about 90 minutes at the most to go through *The Nu ESP Test* from beginning to end, you may find you need to take periodic breaks. If you do, just mark your page and do not peek ahead! When you return, try not to be concerned about how long it takes for an impression to form. Sometimes you will see the best results if you take no longer than about 60 seconds per challenge, and other times, you may need to tune into your mind's "movie" in an unhurried manner.

Try not to be frustrated at the fact that you will be asked questions about things that you can't actually know about. Just open your mind, and let the answer come to you. It's important that you don't let your creativity force what you want to appear, but rather to allow an image to intuitively form in your mind. The following challenges will require that you spend approximately one minute to form written "automatic impressions," in the form of subconscious visual images or feelings (as mentioned at the end of the last section) while addressing each of the questions asked. Do your best to get into the "state of mind" that gives you correct results!

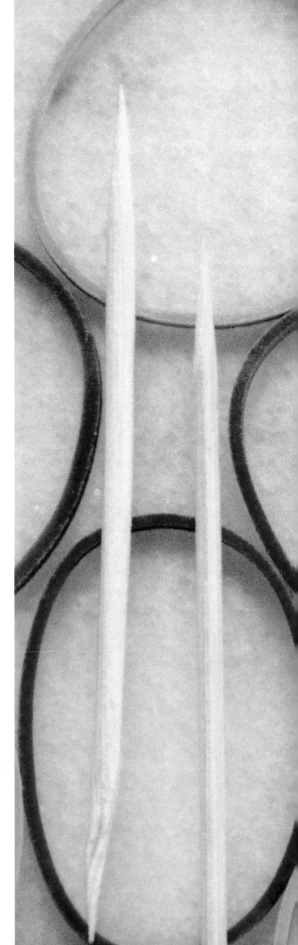

Clear your mind until all you see is one full circle, and a single line pointing straight up and down.

Allow one of the two images to fade, leaving the other to remain in your thoughts.

Now visualize this remaining image as if it were to multiplying into duplicates, and hold that thought for a moment… Finally, without thinking why, visualize yourself looking at a photograph of a "scenic view" of some sort… Write down all your impressions and turn the page.

Photo: Fredde Lieberman

25

If you correctly chose LINES, give yourself TWO blue stars. Now granted, you had a 50/50 chance of getting this one right.

However, if the impression you formed of the "scenic view" in any way resembled a lake or a dock, or something that is significant to this photograph, give yourself THREE green stars.

If you are forming "incorrect impressions," do not worry! Simply clear your mind, and again write down any random thoughts and images that come to you. Later we will review how your overall impressions may have been sensitized while taking this test.

Photo: David Waldman AKA "Pighood" (flickr.com)

White is the only color that represents the entire color spectrum.

Below is a whitish rectangle which you'll focus on for a moment. Think of it as a blank piece of paper.

First allow your mind to change the color of the field from white to a different color, focusing on that color for a moment to confirm your selection. Write down your first thought.

Then imagine a simple geometric shape forms within that colored field. Take note of the shape and allow a specific color to emerge and spread within that shape.

You are now thinking of a specific geometric shape of a certain color within a field of a different color. Write down these impressions along with anything else that randomly comes to your "automatic impressions" and turn the page…

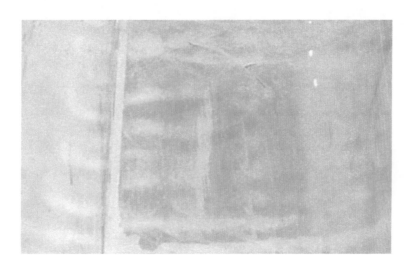

If you thought of a BLUE field, give yourself ONE blue star.

If you picked either the shape of a TRIANGLE or trapezoid, give yourself ONE more blue star.

If you picked the color orange or red within the shape, give yourself ONE more blue star.

If your written impressions in any way felt particularly significant to the image in this photo (ie: if your impressions mention a "warning, obstacle, change of direction" or even matched in appearance a similar image, like a "mountain or volcano") give yourself ONE green star.

Photo: David Waldman AKA "Pighood" (flick.com)

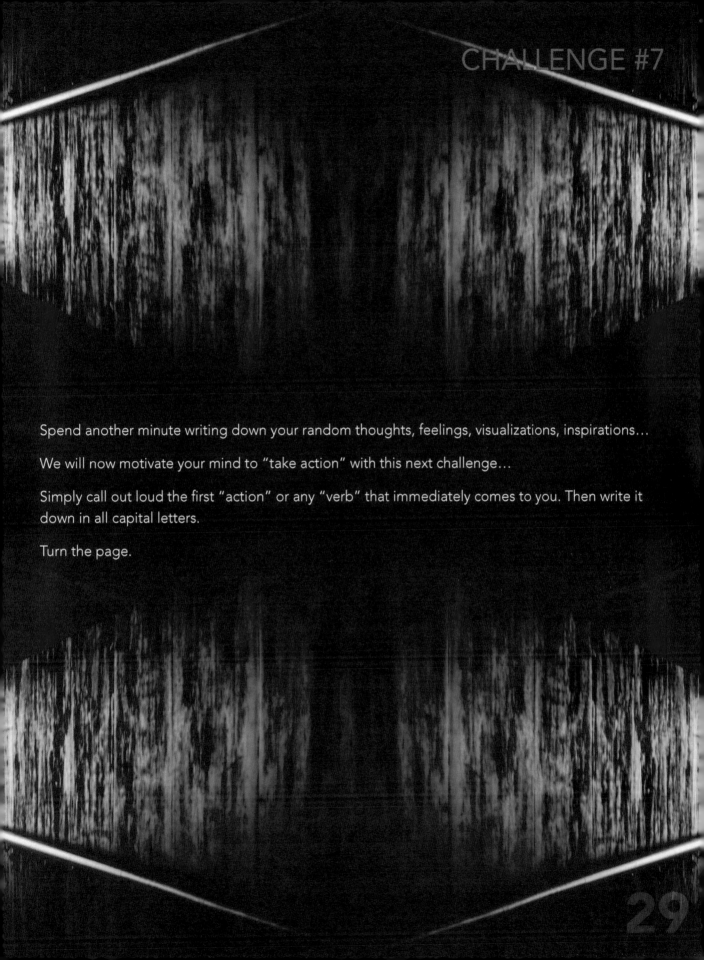

Spend another minute writing down your random thoughts, feelings, visualizations, inspirations...

We will now motivate your mind to "take action" with this next challenge...

Simply call out loud the first "action" or any "verb" that immediately comes to you. Then write it down in all capital letters.

Turn the page.

If you correctly chose RUN or RUNNING, give yourself THREE blue stars.

If your notes mention a tunnel, a silhouette or shadow, or anything that is significantly relative, add ONE green star.

If you actually received an image of running in a tunnel or hallway, give yourself ONE red star.

If you chose a similar pedestrian movement, such as walking, skipping, galloping, etc, give yourself ONE blue star.

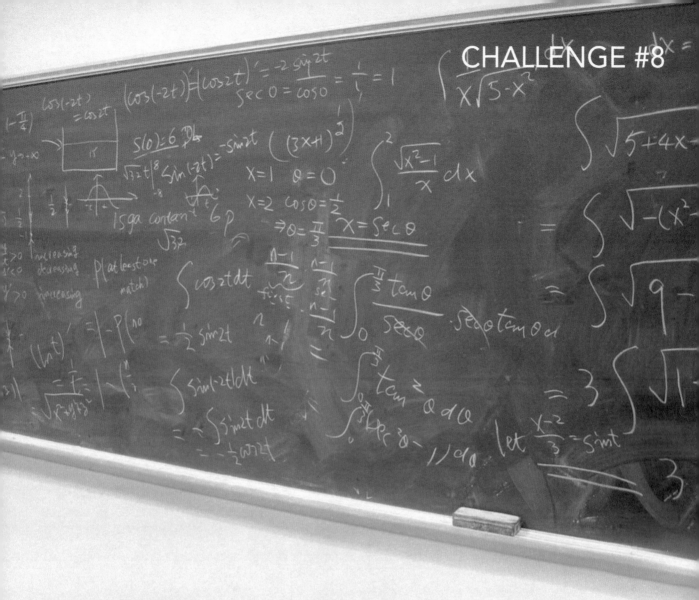

Here's an "odd challenge"…
Follow these instructions carefully:

Think of a two-digit number between 10 and 50,

Both digits within this number must be odd numbers.

And make it so that both digits are different from one another.

Write down your answer then turn the page to see how you did!

This is a photo of 37 37's!

If you picked the number 37 give yourself ONE green star.
If you picked 35 or 39 give yourself TWO blue stars.

Wait a minute, you might be saying, what are the odds here anyway? Between the possible choices 13, 15, 17, 19, 31, 35, 37, and 39, a mere guess would be correct one out of eight times. Skeptics, however, will feel that the reader is inclined to choose the number 37 statistically from numerical popularity. In any case, this is an interesting associative challenge, to see if you responded in the direction of the outcome.

Imagine you are in a darkened theatre, but the rectangular screen in front of you is bright and white.

Allow an image of "something one would see outside" to show up on that mental screen. Allow it to naturally come to you, without trying to impress yourself creatively. Take your most vivid impression based on your "natural knowing" and record it.

Now clear your thoughts again.

Imagine you are back in the darkened theatre. Allow a second distinctly different outdoor image to surface and focus on it. Visualize this image in clear detail before allowing it to fade from view.

Write this down as well. You should have recorded two separate "outdoor impressions."

Photo: David Waldman AKA "Pighood" (flick.com)

If you correctly chose TREE and CAR give yourself TWO green stars.

If you chose one of the two, or thought of "dusk" or a sunset, give yourself ONE green star for each correct guess.

If you thought of something similar such as a forest of trees, a street with cars, or even a rural scene, give yourself ONE blue star for each correlation.

So, how have you been doing so far? If you feel you have been performing well, please continue onto the next chapter. You may be on a roll!

If you feel you haven't been performing well, now is a good time to take a break. Sometimes taking a break allows your brain to refresh and "reset" itself without any extra effort on your part. You can return when you feel the moment is right. Mark your page and don't peek ahead!

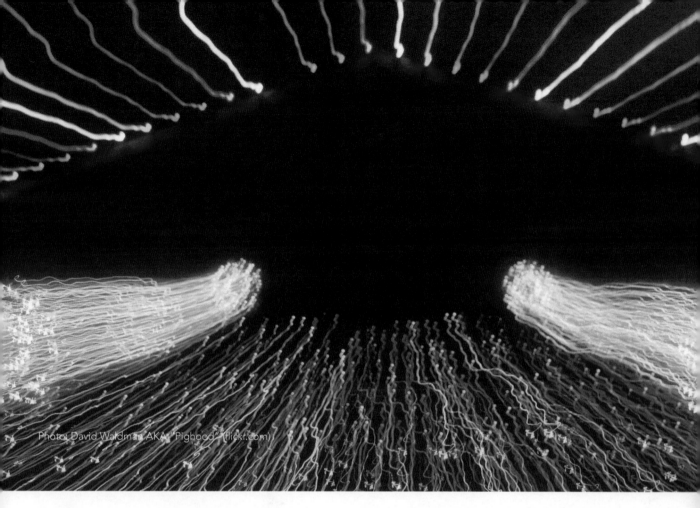

chapter 3:
HOW PSI I AM

Moments of inner-knowing which feel genuine are often attributed to luck or coincidental timing. The difference is that in the experience of the actual moment something about it feels real, or somehow mysteriously guided. In the end, it is only our personal intuition that decides for us if what we experienced was significant, or "just coincidental." The fact is, the significance of synchronistic events and other paranormal topics have been the subject of serious scientific investigation over the past 150 years.

You might be asking yourself right now: "Serious scientific investigation of the paranormal? No way!" But it's true. While skeptics would have you believe there is no science to psi, this is not actually a consensus in the scientific community. While quantum physics and psi studies have lived a dual, but separate, existence for many decades, the gap between the two is closing. It has become part of science's new reality that atomic particles can be affected by mere observation and correlate with one another across enormous distances. One theory gaining momentum among serious scientists is that our brains might be seen as quantum "particle generators:" That is to say, our brains are made up of billions of neurons firing off literally trillions of synapses, and all on an atomic level. With so much atomic stuff happening, inside AND outside our heads, it's not hard to imagine that some particle exchange, signal, or what is called "quantum entanglement," would be happening almost all the time.

While I will not be delving into the spooky nature of quantum physics in this book, you can read all about it in some of the recommendations I include in the "further reading section" at the end of this book. For now, just consider: the next time you are able to complete someone else's thought before they say it out loud, or think of the name of a friend just before they pick up the phone to call you, it might NOT be a simple coincidence!

But will we ever know for sure that a sixth sense actually exists? For now, we can't be 100 percent certain in part because we cannot yet concretely define what a sixth sense is. Only tiny glimpses of this "it" are now being replicated under laboratory conditions, and although the phenomenon is not fully understood, there is sufficient evidence beyond statistical chance to warrant further investigation. A few pioneering serious scientists are going where few others dare to go. Read up on their studies and findings and you will no doubt be impressed at how hard they have worked to construct tests with resultant findings that withstand scientific scrutiny of their peers. It's a small but growing body of work that will eventually transform the way we look at our minds and, indeed, our world.

Everyone's personal experience of psi is their own to explore freely and in any direction they choose.

The following challenges will not require that you write any "automatic impressions" as instructed earlier. Rather develop a natural and fluid pace for yourself as you run through this section quickly while recording your score. Clear your mind of any concerns about proving or disproving anything to yourself as you go through the next set of challenges.

It's not a good pokerhand, but this apparently meaningless hand is perfect for our purposes.

Allow your mind to consider each card before it naturally and sincerely chooses to bring one into significant focus.

Then turn the page...

Photo: Fredde Lieberman

If you correctly chose the FOUR OF HEARTS, give yourself ONE green star.

Imagine these three coins falling one by one. They land next to one another.

Which sides did each coin land on, and in what order?

Turn the page to see your results!

Photo: Fredde Lieberman

If you correctly determined the left to right order of heads and tails, give yourself TWO green stars.

If you were correct in determining there were two heads and one tail but you didn't get the order exactly right, give yourself ONE green star.

If you got any correct head or tail in the correct place give yourself ONE blue star.

Photo: Fredde Lieberman

These cards were created at Duke University in the 1930's for the laboratory testing of ESP.

Look at these five symbols, but let's put the most focus on the CIRCLE. Close your eyes, Let the circle flash in your mind, and call a number out loud between one and 25.

Write down the strongest impression that entered your mind and then turn the page...

Photo: Fredde Lieberman

As you can see, each card on this page correlates to a numerical position, which on the previous page you were asked to focus on any.

If the number you chose corresponds to where the CIRCLE is, give yourself THREE green stars.

If you find that a circle is on a card to either side of the numbered positioned you chose, that's still close! Give yourself ONE green star.

Photo: Fredde Lieberman

Modern playing cards strangely resemble the modern calendar:

1) The two basic colors of a deck of cards, red and black, represent day and night.

2) There are four suits that represent the four seasons to the year.

3) Each suit is divided into 13 values, symbolic of the 13 lunar cycles.

4) The 52 cards represent the 52 weeks in the year.

5) Each value of each suit (from one to 13), when added equals to 364—just one day short of 365 days in a year.

6) There are two "Jokers" that always come with a new deck of cards. One represents the 365th day of the year and the second one is reasoned to symbolize the extra day in February for each "leap year."

7) Furthermore, spelling out all the values and adding up the letters equals to 52 letters!

This time think of any playing card from a deck of 52 cards. This can be any card at all, so long as you feel the choice you made was your own. Write it down.

Now try to completely clear your mind and allow literally any number between 1 and 52 to enter into your thoughts. Write it down.

Turn the page to see how close you came…

Photo: Fredde Lieberman

Photo: Fredde Lieberman

This is not an easy test, and you will have had to truly figure out some way of tuning-in to the cosmic universe to correctly hit on this one.

If you named the correct card at the exact number in this pictured spread, give yourself ONE red star.

If the card you chose is positioned within five cards in either direction of the number you chose, give yourself TWO green stars.

If it's within 10 cards, give yourself TWO blue stars.

44

chapter 4:
PARANORMAL THINKING

Earlier I referenced the difficulty of defining a sixth sense scientifically. But there is a popular consensus on what the definition of ESP (extra sensory perception) is: any kind of ability to perceive outside of what your ordinary five senses tell you. That sounds like a broad category because it is. It is usually mentioned alongside abilities such as telekinesis, clairvoyance, telepathy and other sub-categories. An even broader category of was coined by B.P. Weisner and R.H. Thouless in 1942 to bring together the study of both ESP and Telekinesis (or mind over matter). This is how the word "psi" (pronounced "sigh") came into being.

45

Two categories of psi that consistently fascinate people are mind reading and the ability to contact the dead. It's not hard to see why. Abilities in these two areas, especially as portrayed on TV and in film, would make life pretty different from how we live it. Yet beyond these popular images of psychics and mediums to which we are all exposed, most of us have either had some kind of ESP experience or know someone who feels they have. Most often these personal experiences are discussed only among family and the most trusted of friends. Despite the growing acceptance of psi among ordinary people, the stigma surrounding psi topics created by portions of the scientific and skeptical community often make open discussion problematic.

There are countless times that strange and unexpected synchronicities happen in one's real life. Although these instances are striking and usually hit the odds at a significant margin above chance, it is extremely difficult to duplicate these types of experiences in the laboratory. It takes hundreds to thousands of repeated and inter-related tests, using a generally unorthodox criterion of requirements, among others patience, before one can come to any definitive conclusion about what these findings actually mean. However, recent meta-analysis done to mathematically calculate the odds of most every test in every category of psi over the last 100 to 150 years shows that the average human being has extra-sensory abilities that consistently hit a little above chance.

Skeptics will say here that there is nothing interesting about this. They state that this simply shows us roughly what we already "know": that we are as good as our guesses,

and to tilt a study so that it comes out curiously "above average" is too easy to accomplish by any number of ways. But it's more complicated than that. Just one of many recent astonishing findings: researchers at the Institute of Noetic Sciences found that people have an innate natural ability to sense random frightening images from neutral ones approximately three seconds BEFORE they are flashed on a TV screen! Abilities such as this that have nothing to do with chance are not so easily dismissed. (Refer to the suggested reading list to learn more.)

It is in the consistency of each replication of these studies combined with continued serious testing procedures and data that we will ultimately find further answers to these kinds of questions. This much is certain: the brain is the most complex organ in our body. So much of what we know about the brain only demonstrates how much more we have yet to learn. Many of its functions are not fully understood and remain a true mystery

Keep in mind the purpose of this book is to allow you to begin an open-ended process of personal exploration. Once again I will ask you to clear your mind and prepare to go through the next series of challenges.

"THE BEST WAY TO PREDICT THE FUTURE IS TO CREATE IT."
—ABRAHAM LINCOLN

One of Abraham Lincoln's great quotes was: "The best way to predict the future is to create it."

But President Lincoln had no reason to end his life, so it's fair to believe that his premonition of his death by assassination, just two weeks before his life was taken from him, was not of his conscious intention. Could Abraham Lincoln have experienced "precognitive psi?" Three days prior to his assassination, Abraham Lincoln made specific mention to his wife and a few friends of a strange dream that had affected him:

"About ten days ago, I retired very late... I could not have been long in bed when I fell into a slumber, for I was weary. I soon began to dream… Before me was a catafalque, on which rested a corpse wrapped in funeral vestments. Around it were stationed soldiers who were acting as guards; and there was a throng of people, gazing mournfully upon the corpse, whose face was covered, others weeping pitifully. 'Who is dead in the White House?' I demanded of one of the soldiers, 'The President,' was his answer; 'he was killed by an assassin.' Then came a loud burst of grief from the crowd, which woke me from my dream. I slept no more that night; and although it was only a dream, I have been strangely annoyed by it ever since."

SOURCE: p. 116-117 of Recollections of Abraham Lincoln 1847-1865 by Ward Hill Lamon (Lincoln, University of Nebraska Press, 1994).

CHALLENGE #14

Could you be similarly precognitive? Don't worry, I won't make this next challenge life-threatening. But see if you can guess the right one. Only one of the following famous DC tour sites will be captured on the next page:

1) The White House
2) The Washington Monument
3) The Jefferson Memorial
4) The US Capitol

You don't even need to know what these sites look like. Simply "know," and then turn the page.

Photo: Fredde Lieberman

49

If you correctly chose the world's largest OBELISK, The Washington Monument, give yourself THREE blue stars!

Imagine that you are a film director and you are shooting in one of the following areas of this building for your next scene… Use your intuition, not your judgment! Which would you choose?

1) The staircase
2) The boiler room
3) The rooftop
4) The parking lot

Photo: Fredde Lieberman

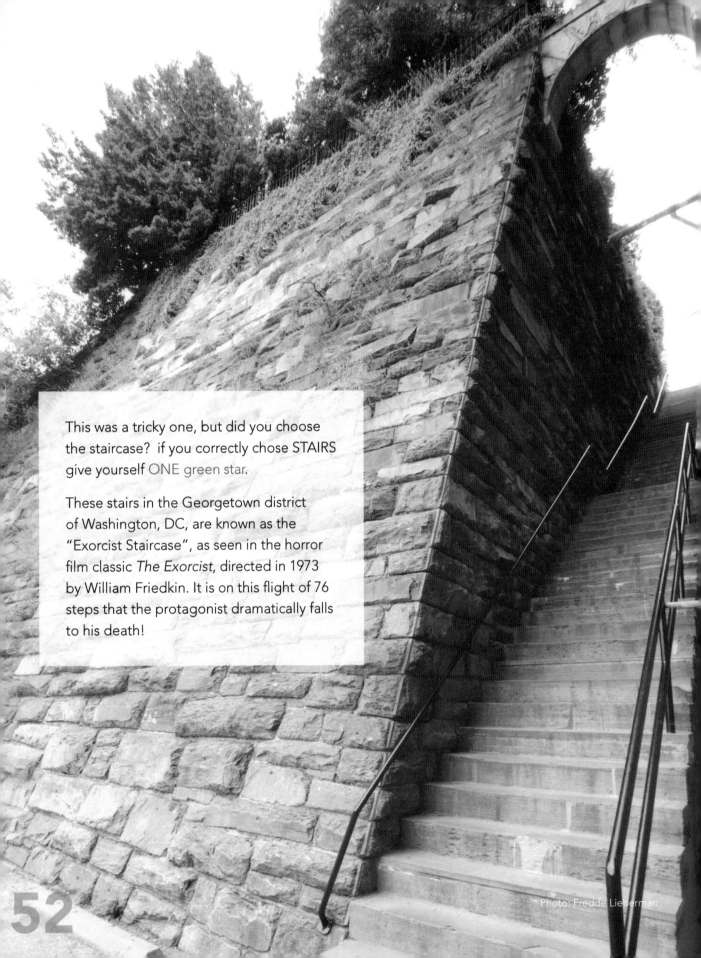

This was a tricky one, but did you choose the staircase? if you correctly chose STAIRS give yourself ONE green star.

These stairs in the Georgetown district of Washington, DC, are known as the "Exorcist Staircase", as seen in the horror film classic *The Exorcist*, directed in 1973 by William Friedkin. It is on this flight of 76 steps that the protagonist dramatically falls to his death!

52

Try not to think too hard about which one to mentally eat before writing it down and turning the page.

Photo: Tanya Thielke

If you guessed POPCORN, give yourself THREE blue stars!

Perhaps your sixth sense is more of a visual sense.
Deliberate over these flowers for a moment, and then imagine
yourself plucking one of them out of the photograph.
Which one was it?

If you thought of the Black Eyed Susan, give yourself THREE blue stars!

You have reached the final of five challenges in this chapter. The preceding challenges give you only a 25% chance of "guessing" the correct choice. If you end up being correct on three of these, you are doing exceptionally well. If you have not been performing well at this point, take a moment to make sure you are comfortable with your methods of contemplation during the meditation and instructions.

This fifth challenge is trickier than you think.

This guy in this photograph is feeling pretty lucky. However, he's married to only one of these four women...

Which of these four women do YOU think he is actually married to? Spend a moment looking each one in the eye and write down which would be your first and second choice. Write your final answers down before turning the page...

Photo: Fredde Lieberman

If your first choice for my friend Matthew Lesko's wife was Wendy, give yourself ONE green star!

If Wendy was your second choice as Matt's potential wife, give yourself TWO blue stars. (I promise not to tell her!)

58

Photo: Fredde Lieberman

Photo: David Waldman AKA "Pighood" (flickr.com)

chapter 5:
FUNNY FEELINGS

As you may have suspected by now, some of the challenges in this book are designed to be easier than others. But I assure you some are also quite difficult! I certainly didn't want to make all the early ones easy. If your aptitude is naturally high, you would still get the immediate gratification of seeing what you are capable of.

I spoke earlier of the difficulty of creating a single perfect test for ESP. However, you may already find yourself hitting remarkably high on your choices. If you are, you're on the right track. But if you are not, it does not mean you are on the "wrong track." This is just another example of the nature of psi experiences. The fact that they are not easily quantifiable does not make them irrelevant or not worthy of further personal investigation. Obviously you already feel this way or you would not have this book in your hands!

Another phenomenon that has fascinated humans from the beginning of their history is the experience of dreaming. This is another area that science has not been able to completely explain or understand. Why do we dream? Does it serve some necessary function in our bodies or minds? These are just some of the questions being explored.

Dreams are strange and interesting experiences. Some people remember them regularly, keep journals about them, and even attempt to manipulate their outcome via various techniques of" lucid dreaming." But listen to any average person describe a dream and you will notice something striking: the description is not just about vivid visual images or a series of bizarre events; there are also strong physical sensations that are experienced, from such basics as "hot" or "cold" to complex tactile sensations like touching or flying. There are also feelings and emotions that seem just as significant to the dream as the events portrayed therein.

The next set of challenges will try to connect with these very basic senses. During each instructional meditation, allow any incoming images to give way to sensations such as those you might experience while dreaming. You might not feel them physically as much as conceptually. As with all the other meditations, try to ascertain that feeling or concept which stands apart from the others. You might want to gently focus on your breath for a few moments before writing down any impressions. As always, while taking notes, remember to include as much detail as possible before turning the page.

Take a deep breath and try to find that "sweet-spot" in your
minds eye… Use your inner-knowing to detect whether
you feel a "hot or cold" feeling from the next photograph.
What do you feel?

Write down either "hot" or "cold" and then turn the page.

Photo: Tanya Thielke

Did you feel hot over cold?
If HOT was your answer, give
yourself TWO blue stars.

Let's try this again, but a little differently…

This time, allow yourself to "feel" whether the next image depicts something rough or smooth. Next, see if you can tune into either a hot or cold sensation.

Write down your two answers. For this challenge, also jot down six or seven automatic impressions of any incoming visualized images before turning the page.

Photo: Freddie Lieberman

If you correctly chose cold and smooth, give yourself TWO green stars.

If you received any significant impressions, such as a winter scene or spiky objects, give yourself ONE more green star.

If one of your two impressions was correct (either smooth OR cold), give yourself ONE blue star.

Before you move on to the next challenge, again, write down any impressions, feelings and images that may be coming to you regardless of how random they might seem. This will help clear your mind and reset your concentration for the next challenge.

Relax and focus your mind. Try again to intuit the next photograph. Do you feel it as "powerful" or "docile?" Also, do you see it as "large" or "small?"

Photo: David Waldman AKA "Pighood" (flickr.com)

If you thought "powerful" and "large," give yourself ONE green star.

If you only thought of one correct answer, give yourself ONE blue star.

If you received any significant impressions such as automobiles, construction vehicles, or trucks, give yourself ONE more green star.

If your impression was that of a "TRAIN" of any kind, give yourself TWO red stars.

7 ▾   **black** ▾   ✂ 📋 📋 | **B** *I* <u>U</u>

These four emoticons are commonly used to convey human expressions. Allow your mind to clear and focus in on which of these four expressions is conveyed in the photograph on the next page. Once you have written down your answer, clear your mind again. Imagine yourself turning the page and seeing either a male or a female face with this expression. Finally, try to determine the approximate age of that person. Make sure that you have recorded all three impressions before turning the page.

If you chose the correct expression, give yourself THREE blue stars.

If you correctly chose female, give yourself TWO blue stars.

If you correctly ascertained this person to be a young adult, give yourself ONE green star.

If you correctly thought of all of the above, give yourself ONE red star.

Photo: D. Sharon. Pruitt (flickr.com)

chapter 6:
SIXTH SENSE

There's an old saying, a disclaimer of sorts, about my craft:

"Mentalism is what allows a performer to combine the five senses, experienced by an audience, in such a way as to create the illusion of a possible sixth sense."

My feeling, however, is that the purpose of performing mentalism has always been more to inspire fascination with this mysterious sixth sense, about which we know so little. Although I am able to control my demonstrations to some degree, I always leave plenty of opportunities for "something real" to take place. Having explored this territory with two decades of experience, I can truly say that I myself am amazed at just how often an unexplained outcome manifests itself.

Photo: David Waldman AKA "Pighood" (flickr.com)

This "ESP" sense that I am referring to cannot be described as simply coming from parts of the actual five senses. It feels like it exists separately somehow. Perhaps it's an actual brain signal or set of signals that somehow crosses into our conscious awareness. This sensitivity to subtle impressions filtered through our mind from unknown places is what I am actually after!

The simple idea behind ESP is that "something" emerges from "nothing." If this is actually possible, there must be a mindset that makes this work the best. But it might not be the same for everyone. In trying to learn about your intuition, take note of which challenges appear to work for you, and what you recall about your mental state when they did. From there, try to remember how you got into that headspace.

I hope you have remained open-minded up to this point and have made notes of your progress without focusing too much on your results. It is important that you continue to stay free of judgment about yourself and your abilities. Much of this test is quite difficult, and if you have performed well on only a few of the challenges, you cannot come to any conclusions just yet!

You are about to go through another set of exercises designed to hone in on what specific kinds of challenges you personally have a knack for. So if you have already found your zone, stay in it! If not, then once again empty your mind and relax. Let those feelings and impressions that stand apart from the rest to guide your choices as you read the instructions for each of the following challenges.

The ability to bend metal with only the powers of the mind has fascinated people for centuries.

Imagine yourself possessing this ability. Visualize one of these six items bending at your command…

Write down which one you bent and turn the page.

Photo: Fredde Lieberman

Give yourself ONE green star if you mentally bent the spoon photographed!

If you didn't, but thought of the other spoon pictured, give yourself TWO green stars.

Scientifically speaking, the "fruit" is the part of the plant that contains seeds, and therefore tomatoes, are technically considered fruit and not vegetables…

Without tomatoes, let's consider other vegetables. Actually, just say the word "vegetable" three times in your mind, and then allow a single vegetable to enter your thoughts as you do this. Write it down.

Now think of taking two dice… roll one in your mind, and note its number. Now roll the other one and note the second number. Add up your two numbers.

You now have a vegetable and a number in your mind.

Photo: Tanya Thielke

If you answered "carrot," give yourself ONE green star.

If you thought of the number SEVEN, give yourself another ONE green star.

Photo: Tanya Thielke

Now let's test your sixth sense for "hearing." Imagine a single musical instrument playing in your mind's ear. One of the instruments listed below is pictured on the next page:

A piano
A flute
A violin
A guitar

Which one do you think it is?

Photo: David Waldman AKA "Pighood" (flickr.com)

Were you thinking of the "flute?" Give yourself THREE blue stars.

Photo: Douglas Moors

Let us now work with sensing human emotions.

The picture on the next page portrays an intense emotion.

Close your eyes and allow yourself to sense what that emotion is. Write down more than one if it helps you zero in on the correct feeling.

Also, see if you receive any incoming impressions regarding anything specific about the image. Write them down if you do.

As soon as a clear impression forms, turn the page.

Photo: D. Sharon Pruitt (flickr.com)

If you correctly thought of joy, excitement or anything similar in energy that relates to this image, give yourself ONE green star.

If you also received anything more specific about the image, such as a person jumping for joy, dancing or a visual element like a sunset or a silhouette, give yourself ONE red star.

If you thought of something similar like being proud, active, or a smiling face, give yourself THREE blue stars.

Photo: D. Sharon Pruitt (flickr.com)

As in the previous challenge, tune into the emotion depicted on the next page. Write down as many impressions as may come to you, until you feel certain about your selection.

In addition, write down any other visual impressions that may form in your mind. Then turn the page.

Image: Tanya Thielke

If any of what you wrote on your list corresponds with this photo in a genuine way, give yourself ONE green star for each matching correlation. THREE green stars in this challenge equals ONE red star!.

80

chapter 7:
AWARENESS

You are about to go through the final challenges in this book. I hope you have been keeping track of your results and taking careful notes!

You may have noticed a certain awareness coming over you during those challenges where your impressions ended up matching the image on the next page. This is the type of awareness that we are trying to develop with *The Nu ESP Test*.

In these final challenges, you will be given the most freedom to trust your strongest incoming feelings or hunches. Though they are not necessarily the "hardest" or "easiest," they are the least confining in their design. I have used the word "challenge" throughout this book, but I did not want you to ever associate that term with a competition or any kind of need to perform well. Hopefully you will have found these to be playful explorations into your mind's ability to perceive things that have not yet been revealed. In this book, these "things" are only photographs. But they could be the key to unlocking your untapped abilities to "know" significant things and events in your life before they happen.

Here are some questions for you to think about regarding your progress so far:

Did you have a sense one way or the other about how "well" you would do? If so, were you correct?

Did you find yourself making adjustments in your internal process to adjust your outcomes? In other words, were you able to find a way of allowing your mind to be more receptive that seemed to work better than another?

Did you find that the speed at which you went through the tests affected the outcome?

Did you perform more accurately at certain types of challenges than others?

Did you do "better" or "worse" as the test went on?

You have had lots of opportunities to think about your results so far and what they might indicate about your current level of intuitive ability. In the section at the end of this book called "Final Thoughts," we will examine some of these important ideas in the context of your actual score, which you will calculate immediately after taking these final challenges.

For now, take a few breaths and focus on your "intuitive awareness." With each instructional meditation, allow the most persistent impressions to move into the foreground and make note of them before moving on.

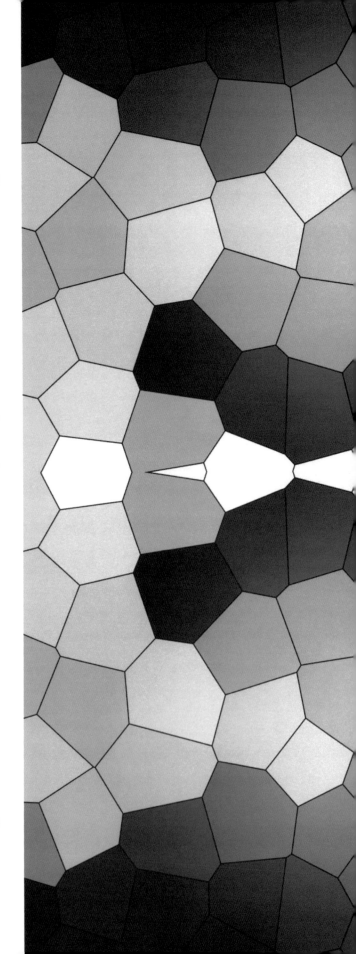

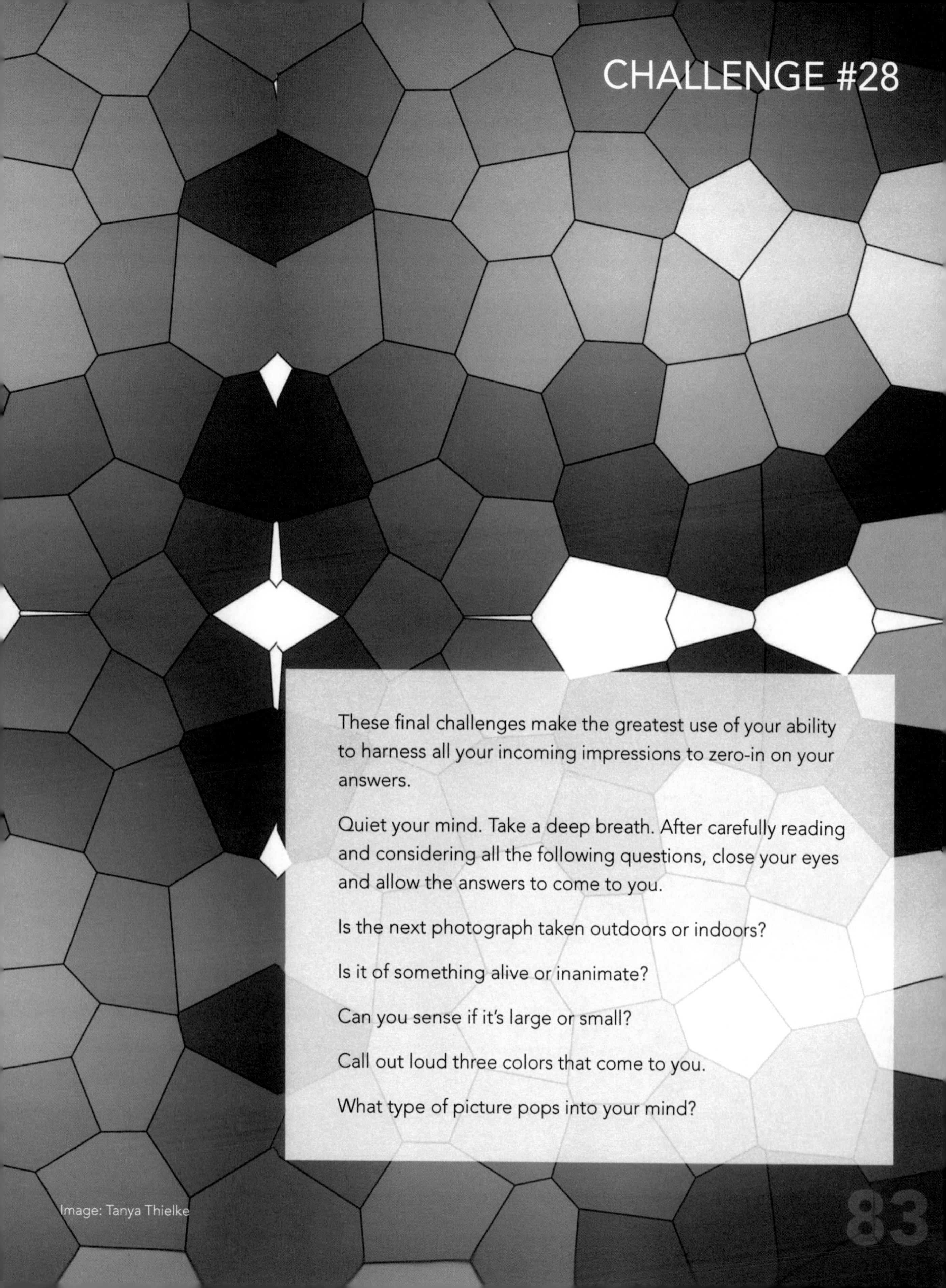

These final challenges make the greatest use of your ability to harness all your incoming impressions to zero-in on your answers.

Quiet your mind. Take a deep breath. After carefully reading and considering all the following questions, close your eyes and allow the answers to come to you.

Is the next photograph taken outdoors or indoors?

Is it of something alive or inanimate?

Can you sense if it's large or small?

Call out loud three colors that come to you.

What type of picture pops into your mind?

Image: Tanya Thielke

83

For the correct location (outdoors,) give youself ONE blue star.

For the correct answer "animate," give youself ONE blue star.

For each correct color, give youself ONE green star.

If you thought of flowers or vegetation, give yourself TWO green stars.

If you chose any insect, give yourself ONE red star.

If you thought of flying or flight, give yourself ONE more red star.

THREE green stars equals ONE red star!

As with the previous challenge, clear your mind and read all questions carefully before closing your eyes to allow incoming impressions and images to form.

You see a piece of furniture.

Is it outdoors or indoors?

Something is resting on it. Is it animate or inanimate?

Can you sense if it is hard or soft?

Finally, tune into three colors.

Write all your answers down before turning the page.

What did you "see?"

If you saw a chair, give yourself ONE green star.

If you correctly chose the location outdoors, give youself ONE blue star.

For the correct choice "inanimate," give youself ONE blue star.

For doll, give yourself ONE red star.

If you thought of something made of fabric or soft like a pillow, give yourself TWO green stars.

For each correct color, give yourself ONE green star.

If any other portion of the image just came to you, such as an American flag, give yourself ONE red star.

This is your final challenge at bringing together your intuitions to divine a complex image.

Allow yourself to tune into four significant colors. Write them down.

Visualize a central figure. Do you see a man or a woman?

Among the animals that do not fly, choose two that are distinctly different from one another other as they appear in your mind.

Write these down.

Of the utensils used to eat and drink, imagine two completely different ones placed before you.

Finally, say the numbers one, two and three out loud to yourself until the most significant moves into your minds foreground.

Make note of all your answers as well as any other incoming impressions, images, feelings and sensations. Then turn the page.

Photo: Fredde Lieberman

For the correct number choice "one," give yourself THREE green stars.

For each correct color choice give, yourself ONE green star.

If you correctly divined three out of the following five: four, red, yellow, green, purple and white, give youself ONE red star.

For the correct choice man, give yourself TWO blue stars.

For any correct animal, give yourself THREE green stars.

For any animal that is close to the ones pictured, such as any feline or reptile, give yourself ONE green star.

For any correct animal, give yourself THREE green stars.

For any animal similar to the ones pictured, feline or reptile, give yourself ONE green star.

If you thought of a knife or a cup, give yourself TWO green stars.

If any of your notes or visual impressions felt significantly noteworthy to the image depicted, give yourself ONE red star.

If you correctly divined the overall composition of the image, or "The Magician" tarot card, give yourself TWO red stars.

This is a tarot card depicting " The Magician." It repre- sents talents, capabilities and a mastery of one's elements. Its underlying message is that one can reach one's full po- tential by taking guidance from one's own intuition to bring about personal transformation.

I thought this was the perfect message to leave you with!

Photo: Fredde Lieberman

your psychic score and what it means

You should now have a sheet of paper with three columns filled with stars and notes of your impressions. But what does any of this actually mean?

Lets begin with the score. Remember, the scoring system relies in part on calculations of your odds at simply guessing the correct answer. For example, a correct guess where the odds are one in two chance, or 50/50 chance, is not impressive, but the unlikelihood of guessing correctly becomes significant where the odds are, say, one in 132. The real test is how you do over a period of time over a large number of tests. Though this book contains a modest amount of challenges (30), it is enough of a sample size to get an overall impression.

Look at your tally sheet. Where are the largest number of stars located?

If your stars are mostly blue, you demonstrated an average amount of psi ability in these tests. These represent odds beyond statistical chance, but not drastically so.

Scoring blue stars in a minimum of FIFTEEN out of the thirty challenges puts you *nicely above average* intuitive potential. TWENTY-FIVE or more blue stars in their column will put you *significantly above average*.

If you have a significant amount of stars in the green column, (TEN+ green stars is impressively above average/ TWENTY+ green stars is extraordinarily impressive) you demonstrated an above average level of psi ability intuition in these tests. The average level of intuition in this realm is actually quite a bit above chance, so moving beyond that puts you in a "very intuitive" category.

If you have ANY stars in the red column, you scored so far enough beyond chance to have *bona fide psi* potential. However, if you have more than FIVE red stars in your column, then you are *truly gifted* psychically.

Again, what does this mean and how can it be useful to you? That depends on how much your test results correlate to your true abilities overall. We all know that not everyone is going to be good at test-taking. We cannot assume that if you scored mostly in the blue star range that you don't possess extraordinary abilities.

So lets take the three levels of PSI abilities we have called blue, green and red and imagine the profile of a person with those varying psychic abilities. See which one describes you best! Does it match your actual score?

Photo: David Waldman AKA "Pighood" (flickr.com)

If you are a "blue star psychic," you probably experience occasional synchronistic events that make you go "hmm." Maybe you called three people the other day who said "I was just thinking of you!", or maybe it's you who regularly knows when your phone is about to ring and who it is going to be. These experiences are probably something you note, but they might not be seen by you as significant life events. You might feel you have a bit of an above-average "read" on people and their qualities, but you have been known to be wrong and so do not use your first impressions as a guide in most situations. Overall, your psychic experiences have been interesting things in your life, and they have made you curious, but you would hesitate to call yourself psychic in general.

If you are a "green star psychic," you probably experience synchronistic events regularly and take note of them. Impressions and intuitions probably form quickly in your mind and you do use them as guides. Your initial impressions about people tend to be uncannily accurate as you get to know them better and you are right enough of the time to use these impressions as guides in your relationships. However, you second guess yourself enough of the time to confuse yourself about how psychic you actually are. While you would hesitate to call yourself psychic even to close friends or family, you have simply had too many experiences not to consider this possibility, even if it makes you uncomfortable.

If you are a "red star psychic," psi experiences likely shape your daily life. Synchronistic and significant events are commonplace to you, and you habitually use them as tools for guidance. You take your impressions about people very seriously and use caution in any relationship with a person about whom you receive an unfavorable read. You may not call yourself a psychic, but your family and friends probably do.

Let us now consider your notes. They may in fact be a source of valuable information to you, and in more ways than one! If you scored high, then they provide a glimpse into the process that you engaged in to get to that particular level of intuitive fluency. If you did not score any stars in over fifteen of the challenges (50% of the test, thus averaging you at under 50% of your intuitive potential), I personally feel that you may still find insights regarding your potential embedded in your written impressions. Ask yourself these questions:

Were you able to feel completely free of your ego or creative mind from "making stuff up?" Were you able to "tune" into a mental-zone that you can recall feeling especially clear to allow your sense of natural-knowing to surface? Understanding this can potentially lead you to your first on-demand encounter with your own ESP abilities!

On those challenges that you did not intuit correctly, do your notes seem different in their expression? In other words, are they less or more descriptive, less or more physical or conceptual? Also, check to see if your "incorrect" impressions actually match future images in other challenges that you had not yet taken. Maybe you were getting ahead of yourself!

Finally, consider your notes as a whole: Even if you scored average, do your notes relate only to *The Nu ESP Test*? Or, as would not be surprising, especially if you achieved a very deep level of concentration and focus, did you receive impressions, images, sensations or feelings that relate to some other issue or concern in your life, such as an unresolved problem, or an important decision you need to make?

The reason I asked you to write down everything is so that at the end of taking the entire test you would also have an accounting of your experience while taking it. Psi experiences often simply feel different from ordinary ones, and the difference can be subtle. The more aware you are of how you feel when you are on to a real hunch, the more you can learn to tap into this potential and actually make a difference in your experience of life.

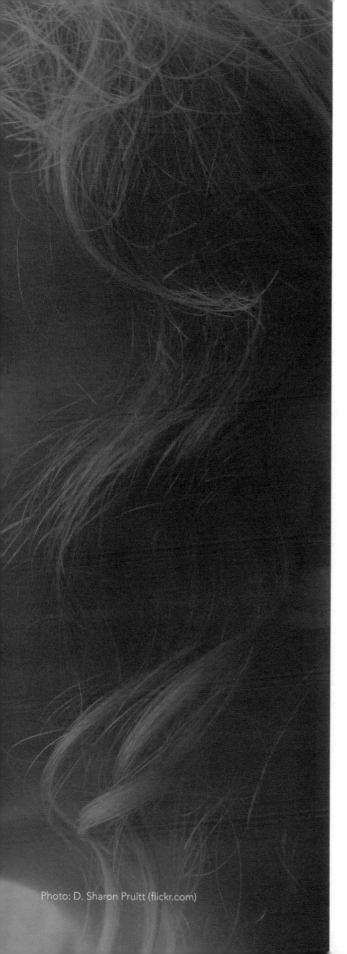

why test your esp?

Your personal reasons for reading this book and taking these tests tell the real story of the human ESP experience. Throughout the ages people have wondered not only about things greater than themselves, but greater things within themselves. Life presents us with challenges and situations in which our awareness, our sense of what is happening, comes into play to help us make important decisions and to guide us in the best direction. School, marriage, career, and health are just a few of the most common areas of life in which our intuitions and the correctness of our perceptions play a crucial role in determining our successes and failures.

Just as there is no single and correct reason to develop your personal intuitive powers, there is no single and correct way to go about it. One of the most effective ways, though, is to begin taking stock of when your actions followed your intuitions towards a positive outcome and when they did not. For example, you may have gotten into a business arrangement with someone you sensed might not be fully reliable, but because you did not want to make a negative assumption, you proceeded with the plan, only to find out later that you were correct about it not being a good deal. It's impossible to act on every single instinct without being wrong some of the time, no matter how good your track record is. But over time, it does become clear that we tend to either listen to our true inner-guides or block them with our second guesses. This is just one type of example, but a very common one.

Another psi experience with great potential for being useful if used responsibly is in fact very common: the sense that something bad is about to happen or has just taken place. These experiences tend to simply come out of nowhere and feel very different from the more ordinary hunch. They are generally intense or at least persistent and have no clear context. People having them often report that until they came to know the event that related to their feeling, they wondered if they might be going mad. Yet just about anyone you might talk to has a family story, or the story of a friend whose family has been touched by some kind of extraordinary experience of the sort that shows how connected loved ones are to each other. These connections might be more than just biological or from simply knowing each other well. They can span great distances, such as the strong feeling of someone's death in another country or they are more immediate, such as sensing strongly that one should simply take a different path to a destination only to find that a fatal accident was avoided. The first of these happened to my wife's mother, the second happened to me.

While one can probably not work on developing this kind of intuition, since it relies on a catastrophic unpredictable event to take place, you can certainly make a decision to listen to such feelings, even if it means possibly being wrong. I'm sure glad I listened to mine, or else I would not even be here to write this book!

Probably the most basic reason for developing a stronger sense of your intuition is to feel more connected to life. Intuition enriches everyday experience, and taking note of moments that seem beyond the ordinary can give us a greater appreciation of our interconnected universe.

In any case, the desire to explore the possibilities of the mind is strong and will remain so for as long as humanity is in existence. There will, however, be a shift in perception, one that will grow from where we now find ourselves, which is informed by the growing amount of evidence that cannot be forever pushed aside by skeptics or the pressures of the mainstream status quo. As we learn more about the brain itself and as our techniques and methods of testing become more refined, the frontier of mind sciences will only expand.

Even in just one lifetime, no individual could ever run out of interesting things to explore about the mind. What better place to start than with your own!

final thoughts

As I'm sure you now understand in a new way from taking these tests, there is no such thing as a final or ultimate test of intuition. Moreover, there is no such thing as a "perfect" scientifically designed test to give you the ultimate answer to the question: Is there really such a thing as controllable ESP?

People have different levels of awareness at different times of their lives, beyond just having "good" and "bad" days for the purposes of testing. The conditions you put yourself in while testing may have also affected your overall score. Finally, your mindset was also a factor. Ideally, you retained an open-minded confidence. In actuality, however, confidence, conditions, or even awareness do not necessarily have to factor when it comes to many examples of genuine uncanny (or psi) experiences. I personally believe that the first step to understanding any ability within yourself is to start with a quiet mind that is free from any tension, distractions or ego, and then begin an inner-dialogue of learning from there.

now what?

You might feel disappointed that now that you have done these tests, you can't use this book anymore since you know the outcomes. I knew you might feel this way! The great thing about the many wonderful images I have collected here is that you can use them to test your friends. Here are some ideas:

Test them over the phone by reading the instructions for each test and letting them know how well they did.

If you are with someone in person, turn your backs to each other and concentrate on a picture. See if they can pick up on a sense of its content.

Here is a synchronicity experiment: With a friend, choose six photos and assign each a number. Have one of a pair of dice available. Ask your friend to choose of one of the photographs, and then roll the single die. Does the number rolled to match the number of your friend's selection? Repeat this test twenty times and you may find some interesting and unexpected results. While you could do this test with any six objects, the photos in this book were chosen because of their distinctive and striking qualities, which stimulate the mind and make the test more fun!

See if you can design your own experiments! The photos in this book provide a nice mental assortment to test such " subconscious sensitivites" for anyone interested.

KEEP YOUR MIND OPEN

There are many easy and fun ways to move beyond this book and open your mind to the world around you.

See if you can affect your ability to find a parking space in a crowded lot or garage by "conscious intention."

Observe how often you actually know who is calling you without looking at the caller ID.

If you're an avid sports fan, see if you have hunches as to when something truly extraordinary is about to happen, such as a home run, a completed pass, or anything that ends up affecting the mood of the crowd watching.

Take note of unusual coincidences or synchronicities.

See how often you meet people with whom you feel you have a genuine connection, and understand how that connection is maintained to create lasting friendships.

suggested reading

- *The Conscious Universe: The Scientific Truth of Psychic Phenomena* by Dean I. Radin

- *Edgar Cayce: An American Prophet* by Sidney D. Kirkpatrick

- *Entangled Minds: Extrasensory Experiences in a Quantum Reality* by Dean I. Radin

- *The ESP Enigma: The Scientfic Case for Psychic Phenomena* by Diane Hennacy Powell, MD

- *Everybody's Guide to Natural ESP: Unlocking The Extrasensory Power of Your Mind* by Ingo Swann and Marilyn Ferguson

- *Limitless Mind: A Guide to Remote Viewing and Transformation of Consciousness* by Russell Targ and Jean Houston

- *Mental Radio: Studies In Consciousness* by Upton Sinclair

- *Mind Games* by Robert Masters and Jean Houston

- *Miracles of Mind: Exploring Nonlocal Consciousness and Spritual Healing* by Russell Targ and Ph.D. Jane Katra

- *Remote Viewers: The Secret History of America's Psychic Spies* by Jim Schnabel

- *Remote Viewing Secrets: A Handbook* by Joseph McMoneagle

"Alain Nu is seriously mental."
  – *Showbiz Magazine*

"He did things that I had never seen before."
  – Mike Weatherford, *Las Vegas Review Journal*

"Physical laws never apply to his wondrous, mysterious stage performance."
  – Stephen Shedd, *Taconic Weekend*

"To watch him is to throw out all the rules of physics. Time and space are malleable in Nu's deft hands."
  – Eric Brace, *The Washington Post*

"Truly mind-boggling... Your work is stunning…"
  – Tim Robinson, Cirque Du Soleil, Mystere, Treasure Island Resort and Casino

"The modest explorer, the gracious and kind tour guide leading the audience into investigations and ultimately mysterious realms. It works beautifully with electric energy, enormous imagination and warm appeal."
  – Donn Murphy, Ph.D., Executive Director, National Theatre

"Many thanks for your participation in helping to create a most memorable Presidential Inaugural evening following President Obama's swearing in. Hearing comments like "That was unbelievable!" and "It happened right in front of us" are certainly impressive. Simply put, you added intrigue, entertainment and class to that memorable evening!"
  – John F. Sommer Jr., Executive Director, *The American Legion*